HPS 984

ELLIOTT CARTER

CANON FOR 4 — HOMAGE TO WILLIAM
(1984)

For Flute, Bb Bass Clarinet,
Violin and Cello

HENDON MUSIC

BOOSEY & HAWKES

AN IMAGEM COMPANY

DISTRIBUTED BY

HAL•LEONARD®
CORPORATION

7777 W. BLUEMOUND RD. P.O. BOX 13819 MILWAUKEE, WI 53213

FOR THE OCCASION OF

SIR WILLIAM GLOCK'S

RETIREMENT FROM

THE BATH FESTIVAL

WHICH ROSE TO SUCH

EMINENCE UNDER HIS

LEADERSHIP, JUNE 3, 1984

PROGRAM NOTE

CANON FOR 4 — HOMAGE TO WILLIAM was written for the occasion of Sir William Glock's retirement from the Bath Festival which rose to such eminence under his leadership.

Following the pattern of many older pieces written by composers to celebrate one of their musical colleagues by making a demonstration of compositional skill, this four-part canon is quite strictly carried out from beginning to end. The flute imitates the cello in inversion, the bass clarinet imitates it in retrograde, and the violin in retrograde inversion. In using this very restricting technique, I have tried to write music that would be interesting and communicative to a listener not preoccupied with its formal devices.

The London Sinfonietta gave the first performance at a celebration for Sir William on June 3, 1984 during the annual Bath Festival in England.

— Elliott Carter

Duration: *ca.* 4 minutes

Parts are available on sale from the publisher (ENB-259)

for Sir William Glock

CANON FOR 4 – HOMAGE TO WILLIAM

Elliott Carter

* sounds major ninth lower

HPS-984

Printed in U.S.A. 1986

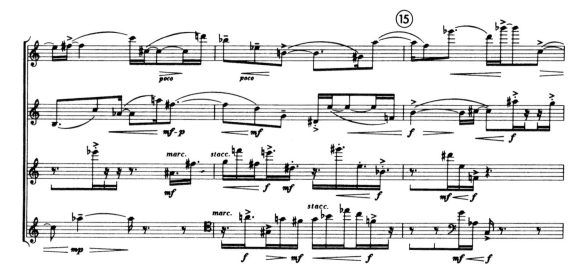

Melodic line to be brought out.

8

12

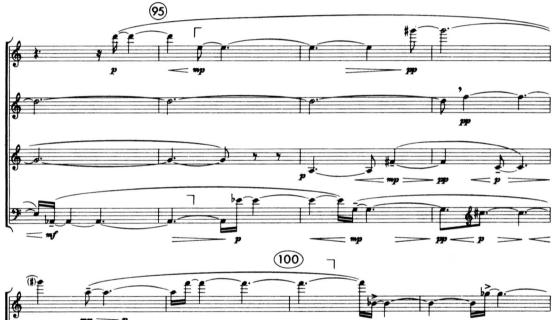

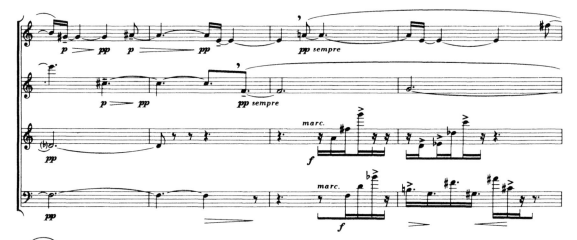

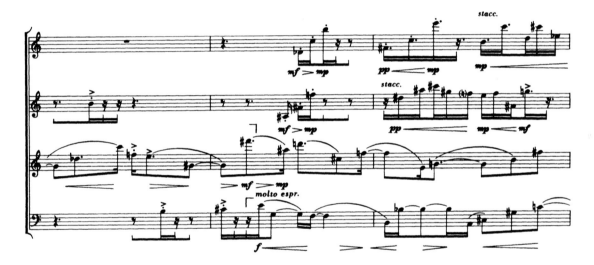

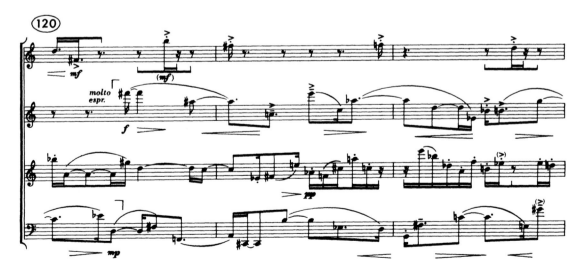

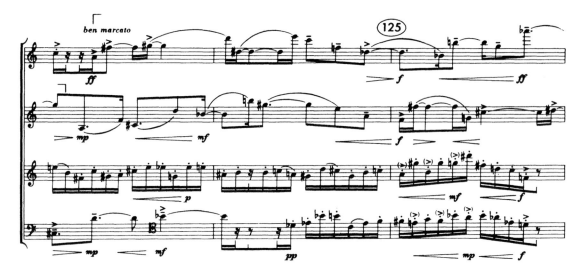

engraved by Geo. McGuire

New York – April 19, 1984